The Teachable Moment
An Educator's Resource

Matthew Goodall

Copyright © 2023 by Matthew Goodall.

No part of this book may be used or reproduced in any form on or by any electronic or mechanical means, including information storage and retrieval systems, without permission in writing from the publisher, except by a reviewer who may quote brief passages in a review.

All rights reserved.

Due to the dynamic nature of the Internet, any web addresses or links contained in this book may have changed since publication and may no longer be valid. The views expressed in this work are solely those of the author and do not necessarily reflect the views of the publisher, and the publisher hereby disclaims any responsibility for them.

This publication is designed to provide accurate and authoritative information in regard to the subject matter covered. It is sold with the understanding that neither the author nor the publisher is engaged in rendering legal, investment, accounting or other professional services. While the publisher and author have used their best efforts in preparing this book, they make no representations or warranties with respect to the accuracy or completeness of the contents of this book and specifically disclaim any implied warranties of merchantability or fitness for a particular purpose. No warranty may be created or extended by sales representatives or written sales materials. The advice and strategies contained herein may not be suitable for your situation. You should consult with a professional when appropriate. Neither the publisher nor the author shall be liable for any loss of profit or any other commercial damages, including but not limited to special, incidental, consequential, personal, or other damages.

Book Cover by MidJourney.

Illustrations by MidJourney, and Matthew Goodall.

First electronic edition.

Book design by Matthew Goodall

ISBN: 978-1-7386047-0-8 (Print)

ISBN: 978-1-7386047-1-5 (E-book)

Published by Matthew Goodall (Aotearoa / New Zealand).

www.matthewgoodall.org

THE TEACHABLE MOMENT COPY

Contents

	Dedication	1
1.	Chapter 1 What is the Teachable Moment?	2
2.	Chapter 2 Knowing the learner.	6
3.	Chapter 3 This isn't difficult.	10
4.	Chapter 4 Remembering the balance.	12
5.	Chapter 5 Support resources for adults.	14
6.	Chapter 6 Colours	18
7.	Chapter 7 Numbers	20
8.	Chapter 8 Shapes	22
9.	Chapter 9 Alphabet	26

10.	Chapter 10 Animals	30
11.	Chapter 11 Imaginative Play	32
12.	Chapter 12 Colours	34
13.	Chapter 13 Numbers	36
14.	Chapter 14 Shapes	38
15.	Chapter 15 Alphabet	42
16.	Chapter 16 Animals	46
17.	Chapter 17 Imaginative Play	48
18.	Chapter 18 Colours	50
19.	Chapter 19 Numbers	52
20.	Chapter 20 Shapes	54
21.	Chapter 21 Alphabet	58
22.	Chapter 22 Animals	62

23.	Chapter 23 Imaginative Play	64
24.	Chapter 24 Image prompts	66
25.	Reviews An Independent Author's Gold	68

Also By Matthew Goodall	69
About the Author	70

To Ritu Bathal of Great Britain,

SuperGirl, Rachel Taylor of Aotearoa

— thank you both for your input and consideration —

and, as always, without measure,

my Mum -

thank you for your love and belief.

Chapter 1

What is the Teachable Moment?

The Miriam Webster online dictionary defines the teachable moment as: 'a time that is favorable for teaching something...'

(https://www.merriam-webster.com/dictionary/teachable%20moment - 24/02/2023)

It's that subtle point in time when you are able to point someone, young or old, in the direction of new knowledge because they're open to it.

Wikipedia defines it as: 'the time at which learning a particular topic or idea becomes possible or easiest.'

(https://en.wikipedia.org/wiki/Teachable_moment - 25/02/2023)

When I asked Chat GPT:

"Please explain the teachable moment, as it relates to early childhood education," it provided this answer:

"The teachable moment is a concept in early childhood education that refers to an opportunity to teach a child a new skill or concept when they are particularly receptive to learning. It is a moment when a child is curious and engaged, and the teacher or caregiver can use that curiosity to introduce new information or reinforce existing knowledge.

Teachable moments can arise at any time during a child's day, but they are particularly common during playtime or when a child is engaged in an activity that captures their interest.

For example, if a child is playing with blocks and asks how to make a particular shape, the adult can use that moment to teach them about shapes and geometry. Alternatively, if a child is excitedly pointing out different animals in a picture book, the teacher can use that moment to teach them about the different types of animals and their habitats.

The key to making the most of teachable moments is to be tuned in to the child's interests and needs, and to be prepared to take advantage of these opportunities as they arise. Teachers and caregivers can use these moments to reinforce existing knowledge, introduce new concepts, and help children develop critical thinking skills. By taking advantage of teachable moments, educators can make learning more engaging and effective, and help children develop a lifelong love of learning."

(9/4/2023)

In both of the examples above, further concepts can be introduced and built on from the child's existing interests.

Chapter 2

Knowing the learner.

I would argue that it's relatively easy for a parent to know what their children are interested in. After all, they (usually), only have a handful of children of their own to think about.

Teachers and educators most likely have a harder job of remembering 30+ different students and their current focus (even worse when children often decide that blue is their favourite colour one day, then red the next!)

Many schools and early childhood facilities maintain diaries or progress notes that offer a snapshot of how each child is learning and growing. These can be invaluable tools to note what the current interests are, and for adults to refer to so that opportunities aren't missed.

One of the models of early childhood devlopment is called scaffolding, which is very basically the idea that people in a child's life provide a structure around a child (a scaffold), that allows the child to 'stand' with this support until they learn the skill for themselves.

It was proposed by the Russian psychologist Lev Vygotsky in the late 1920's, that children will learn more effectively with the help of adults or other skilled peers if they are attempting a task beyond their current ability.

Quite simply put, if the adult / other children can role model the new skill, and provide the child with the space to continue to try it for themselves, it's expected that with time and practice, the child will be able to master it.

For example, a small child is attempting to stack blocks into a tower but can't balance it properly. An adult or older child can show them how to place it so it will stay standing.

This might require a number of demonstrations, and usually over a period of time. At some point, the child should begin to show a greater level of skill, at which point we can step back and simply offer encouragement.

In this example, while the child is engaged, it's possible to expand on the learning that they're engaged with – you could count ('One block, two blocks...); discuss colours ('The brown block, the yellow block – how many blue blocks are there?) etc.

This is all absolutely about knowing the child and their capacity for this extra extension, as well as what they are interested in.

Chapter 3

This isn't difficult.

Knowing the children in your care isn't usually a hard task.

For your own children it can be as simple as observing which books they read, shows they watch, games they play, and toys they play with.

For educators it's about watching your students' interactions – who do they play with the most, what do they like to play with, what activities do they engage with?

"Be intentional and look for teachable moments." (Marybeth Hicks, Teachable Moments, published by Howard Books, 2015).

This isn't new thinking, and definitely isn't rocket science.

The teachable moment isn't a new thing, and it's not something difficult. Our parents and grandparents have been doing it for generations.

Nursery rhymes taught us about music, ryhthm, language, counting. Play taught us how to interact with the world around us. Art and music unlocked our imaginations in other ways.

All of these things have the potential to be 'added to.'

Chapter 4

Remembering the balance.

I would like to take a moment for us to pause and just remember that childhood isn't just about learning and making the most of every teaching moment.

Childhood is also, and should also be, about the joy and magic of discovery.

Splashing in the waves at the beach, climbing trees, throwing and kicking a ball in the back yard or at the park.

Not everything in life needs to be a 'lesson.'

If you're at the beach and your child starts to pick up shells you can ask them which ones they like. If their answer offers an opportunity to talk about shapes, colours or something else, then you can consider that, but equally, it might just be the chance to enjoy the delight on their face as they discover for themself.

Life shouldn't be a series of memories of always being 'taught' something, it should be a time to experience and remember happily.

Chapter 5

Support resources for adults.

Remember, children are often fascinated with the type of things that adults usually prefer not to talk about – poos, fat people, curse words. The trick around these is to skip over the embarrassing part and focus on a 'safe' part.

For example: Your child is in the supermarket and loudly declares, "My poos are brown!"

You smile sweetly at them (probably take a deep breath), and say, "They are. Poos starts with the letter 'p.' What other things start with the letter 'p'?"

Hopefully they'll play along, and you can get back to hiding in the next aisle away from all the other parents who are quietly laughing.

Every concept that a child learns can be linked into another, so that you can extend on their learning, right in the moment that they're engaged with you.

You might be talking about the shape of a window: you can ask what letter 'window' starts with; what colour it is; what shape etc.

If your child prefers to 'do' instead of just talking (hands-on learning), you can encourage them to draw or make the thing with blocks, play dough and so on.

Each of the resources in the following pages has been designed to be as simple as possible, not because I think that adults don't know simple things like colours, but because life is full of many complicated things that we have to keep track of, and sometimes it's the 'little' things that slip our minds.

It isn't a comprehensive list, but is just a starting point to help you support the children in your life.

This has been deliberately set out as a type of workbook so that you can deface it to your heart's content.

I encourage you to write in it, make notes about what works best for you, and your children.

Each of these resource pages are included 3 times (as families typically tend to have up to 3 children).

I need to point out that this booklet is designed specifically with 'educational' aspects in mind. However, the principles of being alert to the teachable moment apply just as much to any other concept that you want your child to learn and grow into – good manners, sharing, helpfulness, independence etc.

Also, parents and caregivers these days are concerned about the amount of time children spend on electronic devices.

Don't forget about trips to the zoo, libraries, parks, museums. Even going to the supermarket or taking a walk around the block offers opportunities to talk about the world around us, and engage them in the things that interest them.

If you want more copies of individual pages you can download these at: https://www.matthewgoodall.org/tmresources

For educators, if you want workbooks, already set up for the children in your care (in groups of 10), you can order these through your usual retailers.
The title and ISBN are:
The Teachable Moment: An Educator's Workbook.

ISBN : 978-1-7386047-2-2 (print) / 978-1-7386047-3-9 (E-Book)

Chapter 6

Colours

What is your child's favourite colour? _____

Primary colours are red, blue, and yellow.

Secondary colours are purple, green, and orange.

Red + blue = purple.

Blue + yellow = green.

Yellow + red = orange.

Red + white = pink.

Black is no colour.

White is all colours – *if you have a prism or a crystal you can show how the light breaks up into a rainbow.*

Black + white = grey.

Rainbow colours, in order: Red; Orange; Yellow; Green; Blue; Indigo; Violet

What letter does THEIR FAVOURITE COLOUR _____ start with?

What other things start with that letter?

How many things can you see that start with (the first letter of the favourite colour)?

What COLOUR _____ things do you like to eat?

(If the favourite colour is a **primary colour**):
What colour do you get if you mix
THEIR FAVOURITE COLOUR _____ and ANOTHER COLOUR?

(If the favourite colour is a **secondary colour**):
What colours do you mix to make THEIR FAVOURITE COLOUR _____ ?

Can you think of any songs about THEIR FAVOURITE COLOUR _____ ?

Encourage them to draw things in THEIR FAVOURITE COLOUR.

Chapter 7

Numbers

For young children, counting should be a reasonably simple task, starting with very basic and working their way up.

How many tummies do you have? *(The answer is one, even if they do seem to eat like they have 2!)*

How many necks?

How many backs?

How many hands do you have?

How many legs / eyes / ears etc?

How many thumbs?

How many fingers? *(It's up to you if you count thumbs along with the fingers)*

This is where you can start to show how different groups can still make the same number (eg. 2 fingers + 2 fingers, or, 3 fingers + 1 finger, or, 4 fingers – all add up to 4).

A song like BINGO is good for learning about the sequence, clapping as each letter of the name is replaced.

There are numerous other songs about counting (I'm *not* thinking of '99 bottles of pop on the wall'!) You can find many examples online to sing along with.

If your child is interested in animals, count how many eyes, legs, different colours etc. they have.

Older children may be able to start to discuss the letters that numbers start with (One is 'o' – even though it sounds like a 'w'; Two is 't' etc).

You can encourage children to draw or write the numbers, draw groups of objects (eg. cars, animals), that have a specific number – one car, two dogs etc.

They may prefer to count physical objects – how many toy cars, how many books, how many cookies (and then you can talk about how many things have been subtracted!)

Chapter 8

Shapes

Knowing which shapes your child might be interested in can help you be on the look out for them in everyday life.

If they particularly like physical play you can encourage them to make, build or draw different shapes.

Here are a few examples.

- **Circles:**

- Eyes

- Your hand/s can make small and big circle shapes

- Pot plant containers
- Wheels.

- **Squares:**

- Windows
- Dice
- Chocolate squares
- Cakes

- **Rectangles:**

- Doors
- Microwaves
- Windows
- Books

- **Triangles:**

- Pizza slice
- Pyramid
- Your hands can make triangle shapes

- The roof of a house

- **Ovals:**

- Eggs

- Football

- Some mirrors

- Avocado

- **Hexagons (6 sides):**

- Honeycomb / Bee hive

- Bolt

- Floor tiles

- The pattern on a soccer ball

- **Octagons (8 sides):**

- Stop sign

- Floor tiles

- Jewellery

- Clock face

Chapter 9

Alphabet

Children often love to sing the alphabet song, and this can be a crucial part of learning.

Ways to extend on it can be to ask, "What can you think of that starts with 'A'?" etc.

Ask them to draw. If they suggest an animal you can talk about the sounds they make, or pretend to be one (eg. a rabbit hopping).

Here are a few suggestions of each letter to help get you started:

A: Apple; Aeroplane; Ant

B: Ball; Baby; Blue

C: Cat; Car; Caravan

D: Dog; Duck; Doll

E: Elephant; Egg; Eye

F: Fish; Frog; Fairy

G: Goat; Ghost; Gold

H: Hippopotamus; Hair; Home

I: Ice Cream; Igloo; Iris (coloured part of the eye)

J: Jump; Jeans; Jelly

K: Kangaroo; Koala; Key

L: Love; Lion; Light

M: Man; Moon; Mouse

N: Necklace; Noodles; Newspaper

O: Orange; Opossum; Oven

P: Purple; Princess; Party

Q: Queen; Quail; Quilt

R: Rabbit; Rainbow; Robot

S: Sun; Spaghetti; Soccer

T: Tree; Tiger; Train

U: Umbrella; Unicorn; Ukelele

V: Violin; Volcano; Vegetables

W: Whale; Water; Walrus

X: Xylophone; X-ray; Xenopus (a type of frog)

Y: Yellow; Yoga; Yacht

Z: Zebra; Zucchini; Zip

Chapter 10

Animals

What is your child's favourite animal? _____

What colour / colours is it?

What letter does it start with?

How many legs does it have?

What does it eat?

What letter does that food start with?

Encourage them to draw the animal – in real colours and imaginative ones.

What songs might include this animal?

Chapter 11
Imaginative Play

Children love to play, and love to play pretend.

Whether they are in the sandpit, climbing trees, building pillow and blanket forts or playing with blocks, there are so many ways to drop in a quick little moment of learning.

The following are only a set of starters to prompt you.

- **In the sandpit:**
- What colour is the sand?
- What letter does that start with?

- How does it feel?

- **Climbing trees:**

- What colour is the tree? leaves?

- What letter does that start with?

- Can you see anything hiding in the tree? (insects, birds etc).

- **Building forts:**

- How many pillows have you used?

- What shape are they?

- What colours are they?

- **Blocks:**

- What are you building?

- What letter does that start with?

- How many blocks have you used?

Chapter 12

Colours

What is your child's favourite colour? _____

Primary colours are red, blue, and yellow.

Secondary colours are purple, green, and orange.

Red + blue = purple.

Blue + yellow = green.

Yellow + red = orange.

Red + white = pink.

Black is no colour.

White is all colours – *if you have a prism or a crystal you can show how the light breaks up into a rainbow.*

Black + white = grey.

Rainbow colours, in order: Red; Orange; Yellow; Green; Blue; Indigo; Violet

What letter does THEIR FAVOURITE COLOUR _____ start with?

What other things start with that letter?

How many things can you see that start with (the first letter of the favourite colour)?

What COLOUR _____ things do you like to eat?

(If the favourite colour is a **primary colour**): What colour do you get if you mix THEIR FAVOURITE COLOUR _____ and ANOTHER COLOUR?

(If the favourite colour is a **secondary colour**): What colours do you mix to make THEIR FAVOURITE COLOUR _____ ?

Can you think of any songs about THEIR FAVOURITE COLOUR _____ ?

Encourage them to draw things in THEIR FAVOURITE COLOUR.

Chapter 13

Numbers

For young children, counting should be a reasonably simple task, starting with very basic and working their way up.

How many tummies do you have? *(The answer is one, even if they do seem to eat like they have 2!)*

How many necks?

How many backs?

How many hands do you have?

How many legs / eyes / ears etc?

How many thumbs?

How many fingers? *(It's up to you if you count thumbs along with the fingers)*

This is where you can start to show how different groups can still make the same number (eg. 2 fingers + 2 fingers, or, 3 fingers + 1 finger, or, 4 fingers – all add up to 4).

A song like BINGO is good for learning about the sequence, clapping as each letter of the name is replaced.

There are numerous other songs about counting (I'm *not* thinking of '99 bottles of pop on the wall'!) You can find many examples online to sing along with.

If your child is interested in animals, count how many eyes, legs, different colours etc. they have.

Older children may be able to start to discuss the letters that numbers start with (One is 'o' – even though it sounds like a 'w'; Two is 't' etc).

You can encourage children to draw or write the numbers, draw groups of objects (eg. cars, animals), that have a specific number – one car, two dogs etc.

They may prefer to count physical objects – how many toy cars, how many books, how many cookies (and then you can talk about how many things have been subtracted!)

Chapter 14

Shapes

Knowing which shapes your child might be interested in can help you be on the look out for them in everyday life.

If they particularly like physical play you can encourage them to make, build or draw different shapes.

Here are a few examples.

- **Circles:**
- Eyes
- Your hand/s can make small and big circle shapes

- Pot plant containers
- Wheels.

- **Squares:**

- Windows
- Dice
- Chocolate squares
- Cakes

- **Rectangles:**

- Doors
- Microwaves
- Windows
- Books

- **Triangles:**

- Pizza slice
- Pyramid
- Your hands can make triangle shapes

- The roof of a house

- **Ovals:**

- Eggs

- Football

- Some mirrors

- Avocado

- **Hexagons (6 sides):**

- Honeycomb / Bee hive

- Bolt

- Floor tiles

- The pattern on a soccer ball

- **Octagons (8 sides):**

- Stop sign

- Floor tiles

- Jewellery

- Clock face

Chapter 15

Alphabet

Children often love to sing the alphabet song, and this can be a crucial part of learning.

Ways to extend on it can be to ask, "What can you think of that starts with 'A'?" etc.

Ask them to draw. If they suggest an animal you can talk about the sounds they make, or pretend to be one (eg. a rabbit hopping).

Here are a few suggestions to help get you started:

A: Apple; Aeroplane; Ant

B: Ball; Baby; Blue

C: Cat; Car; Caravan

D: Dog; Duck; Doll

E: Elephant; Egg; Eye

F: Fish; Frog; Fairy

G: Goat; Ghost; Gold

H: Hippopotamus; Hair; Home

I: Ice Cream; Igloo; Iris (coloured part of the eye)

J: Jump; Jeans; Jelly

K: Kangaroo; Koala; Key

L: Love; Lion; Light

M: Man; Moon; Mouse

N: Necklace; Noodles; Newspaper

O: Orange; Opossum; Oven

P: Purple; Princess; Party

Q: Queen; Quail; Quilt

R: Rabbit; Rainbow; Robot

S: Sun; Spaghetti; Soccer

T: Tree; Tiger; Train

U: Umbrella; Unicorn; Ukelele

V: Violin; Volcano; Vegetables

W: Whale; Water; Walrus

X: Xylophone; X-ray; Xenopus (a type of frog)

Y: Yellow; Yoga; Yacht

Z: Zebra; Zucchini; Zip

Chapter 16
Animals

What is your child's favourite animal? _____

What colour / colours is it?

What letter does it start with?

How many legs does it have?

What does it eat?

What letter does that food start with?

Encourage them to draw the animal – in real colours and imaginative ones.

What songs might include this animal?

Chapter 17

Imaginative Play

Children love to play, and love to play pretend.

Whether they are in the sandpit, climbing trees, building pillow and blanket forts or playing with Lego, there are so many ways to drop in a quick little moment of learning.

The following are only a set of starters to prompt you.

- **In the sandpit:**

  - What colour is the sand?

  - What letter does that start with?

- How does it feel?

- **Climbing trees:**

- What colour is the tree? leaves?

- What letter does that start with?

- Can you see anything hiding in the tree? (insects, birds etc).

- **Building forts:**

- How many pillows have you used?

- What shape are they?

- What colours are they?

- **Lego:**

- What are you building?

- What letter does that start with?

- How many blocks have you used?

Chapter 18

Colours

What is your child's favourite colour? _____

Primary colours are red, blue, and yellow.

Secondary colours are purple, green, and orange.

Red + blue = purple.

Blue + yellow = green.

Yellow + red = orange.

Red + white = pink.

Black is no colour.

White is all colours – *if you have a prism or a crystal you can show how the light breaks up into a rainbow.*

Black + white = grey.

Rainbow colours, in order: Red; Orange; Yellow; Green; Blue; Indigo; Violet

What letter does THEIR FAVOURITE COLOUR _____ start with?

What other things start with that letter?

How many things can you see that start with (the first letter of the favourite colour)?

What COLOUR _____ things do you like to eat?

(If the favourite colour is a **primary colour**): What colour do you get if you mix THEIR FAVOURITE COLOUR _____ and ANOTHER COLOUR?

(If the favourite colour is a **secondary colour**): What colours do you mix to make THEIR FAVOURITE COLOUR _____ ?

Can you think of any songs about THEIR FAVOURITE COLOUR _____ ?

Encourage them to draw things in THEIR FAVOURITE COLOUR.

Chapter 19

Numbers

For young children, counting should be a reasonably simple task, starting with very basic and working their way up.

How many tummies do you have? *(The answer is one, even if they do seem to eat like they have 2!)*

How many necks?

How many backs?

How many hands do you have?

How many legs / eyes / ears etc?

How many thumbs?

How many fingers? *(It's up to you if you count thumbs along with the fingers)*

This is where you can start to show how different groups can still make the same number (eg. 2 fingers + 2 fingers, or, 3 fingers + 1 finger, or, 4 fingers – all add up to 4).

A song like BINGO is good for learning about the sequence, clapping as each letter of the name is replaced.

There are numerous other songs about counting (I'm *not* thinking of '99 bottles of pop on the wall'!) You can find many examples online to sing along with.

If your child is interested in animals, count how many eyes, legs, different colours etc. they have.

Older children may be able to start to discuss the letters that numbers start with (One is 'o' – even though it sounds like a 'w'; Two is 't' etc).

You can encourage children to draw or write the numbers, draw groups of objects (eg. cars, animals), that have a specific number – one car, two dogs etc.

They may prefer to count physical objects – how many toy cars, how many books, how many cookies (and then you can talk about how many things have been subtracted!)

Chapter 20

Shapes

Knowing which shapes your child might be interested in can help you be on the look out for them in everyday life.

If they particularly like physical play you can encourage them to make, build or draw different shapes.

Here are a few examples.

- **Circles:**
- Eyes
- Your hand/s can make small and big circle shapes

- Pot plant containers
- Wheels.

- **Squares:**

- Windows
- Dice
- Chocolate squares
- Cakes

- **Rectangles:**

- Doors
- Microwaves
- Windows
- Books

- **Triangles:**

- Pizza slice
- Pyramid
- Your hands can make triangle shapes

- The roof of a house

- **Ovals:**

- Eggs

- Football

- Some mirrors

- Avocado

- **Hexagons (6 sides):**

- Honeycomb / Bee hive

- Bolt

- Floor tiles

- The pattern on a soccer ball

- **Octagons (8 sides):**

- Stop sign

- Floor tiles

- Jewellery

- Clock face

Chapter 21

Alphabet

Children often love to sing the alphabet song, and this can be a crucial part of learning.

Ways to extend on it can be to ask, "What can you think of that starts with 'A'?" etc.

Ask them to draw. If they suggest an animal you can talk about the sounds they make, or pretend to be one (eg. a rabbit hopping).

Here are a few suggestions to help get you started:

A: Apple; Aeroplane; Ant

B: Ball; Baby; Blue

C: Cat; Car; Caravan

D: Dog; Duck; Doll

E: Elephant; Egg; Eye

F: Fish; Frog; Fairy

G: Goat; Ghost; Gold

H: Hippopotamus; Hair; Home

I: Ice Cream; Igloo; Iris (coloured part of the eye)

J: Jump; Jeans; Jelly

K: Kangaroo; Koala; Key

L: Love; Lion; Light

M: Man; Moon; Mouse

N: Necklace; Noodles; Newspaper

O: Orange; Opossum; Oven

P: Purple; Princess; Party

Q: Queen; Quail; Quilt

R: Rabbit; Rainbow; Robot

S: Sun; Spaghetti; Soccer

T: Tree; Tiger; Train

U: Umbrella; Unicorn; Ukelele

V: Violin; Volcano; Vegetables

W: Whale; Water; Walrus

X: Xylophone; X-ray; Xenopus (a type of frog)

Y: Yellow; Yoga; Yacht

Z: Zebra; Zucchini; Zip

Chapter 22

Animals

What is your child's favourite animal? _____

What colour / colours is it?

What letter does it start with?

How many legs does it have?

What does it eat?

What letter does that food start with?

Encourage them to draw the animal – in real colours and imaginative ones.

What songs might include this animal?

Chapter 23

Imaginative Play

Children love to play, and love to play pretend.

Whether they are in the sandpit, climbing trees, building pillow and blanket forts or playing with Lego, there are so many ways to drop in a quick little moment of learning.

The following are only a set of starters to prompt you.

- **In the sandpit:**
- What colour is the sand?
- What letter does that start with?

- How does it feel?

- **Climbing trees:**

- What colour is the tree? leaves?

- What letter does that start with?

- Can you see anything hiding in the tree? (insects, birds etc).

- **Building forts:**

- How many pillows have you used?

- What shape are they?

- What colours are they?

- **Lego:**

- What are you building?

- What letter does that start with?

- How many blocks have you used?

Chapter 24

Image prompts

Most of the images used I created in MidJourney.

In the interests of fairness, transparency and giving credit where credit is due, the following are the prompts I used to create them.

Cover: cartoon image young children with their back to camera, playing together with multicoloured blocks --s 750 --niji 5

Chapter 1: child standing at a blackboard chalk in one hand --s 750 --niji 5

Chapter 2: cartoon of classroom of young children sitting at desks --s 750 --niji 5

Chapter 3: cartoon rocket science --s 750 --niji 5

Chapter 4: cartoon two children play on a blue and yellow inflatable seesaw, in the style of spirals and curves, associated press photo, traincore, prairiecore, steel/iron frame construction, soft-edged, felt creations --ar 10:7 --s 750 --niji 5 *(I edited this image in ProCreate)*

Chapter 5: cartoon box filled with pens, coloured pencils, paper, string, erasers, a ruler, paper clips --s 750 --niji 5

Chapter 6: photorealistic rainbow above tree, national geographic --s 750 --v 5.1

Chapter 7: *I created this image in ProCreate*

Chapter 8: *I created this image in ProCreate*

Chapter 9: cartoon plane on white background --s 750 --niji 5

cartoon ball on white background --s 750 --niji 5

cartoon duck on white background --s 750 --niji 5

cartoon ice cream on white background --s 750 --niji 5

cartoon moon on white background --s 750 --niji 5

disney style princess dressed in pastel yellow and pastel blue ball gown --s 750 --niji 5

cartoon rabbit on white background --s 750 --niji 5

cartoon male unicorn on white background --s 750 --v 5.1

I merged all these images in ProCreate

Chapter 10: cartoon horse, dog, cat, cow, penguin, whale, frog scattered on white background --s 750 --niji 5

Chapter 11: children playing with imagination --s 750 --niji 5

Reviews

An Independent Author's Gold

Reviews are like gold – they let other people know that you've found something valuable, and help authors to get noticed in the middle of the bookshelves.

If you've found this booklet to be helpful I'd really appreciate it if you could write a couple of lines to review it, and post it wherever you got your copy.

Thank you.

Also By Matthew Goodall

Te Kōrero o te Moko Kauae – The Story of the Moko Kauae
(bilingual: Māori-English)

I Love You To My Heart

Hickory Hickory Dock – A Counting Rhyme

Wagging His Tail Behind Him

Ka Aroha Au I A Koe Ki Tāku Ngakau
(I Love You To My Heart – Māori)

We All Say Goodnight

The Twelve Days of Christmas

I Wish That I Could Have Ice Cream Every Day

I Te Waokū Pōuriuri – In The Dark Dark Woods
(with Raymond Peeti – bilingual: Māori-English)

Taniwha's Terrors

About the Author

A disability support worker, and former teacher, Matthew has been reading and writing since before he started school. His first story was mercilessly edited by his parents, and in between fits of laughter, he learned how creative words and descriptions can bring stories to life.

He has a passion for books and sharing stories that will uplift, teach, and transport you to magical places. If you can share a laugh along the way, all the better!

From Aotearoa/New Zealand, he loves weaving in aspects of his home and mythical elements to his stories.

He shares his life with his long-suffering partner, and their Frenchie, Max.

Keep in touch.

Sign up for a monthly newsletter at:

https://www.matthewgoodall.org/

Instagram:

matthewgoodallauthor

Facebook:

https://www.facebook.com/MatthewGoodallAuthorNZ

www.ingramcontent.com/pod-product-compliance
Lightning Source LLC
Chambersburg PA
CBHW042120100526
44587CB00025B/4126